D0689755

The German Americans

PEG ASHBROCK

WE CAME TO AMERICA

MASON CREST PUBLISHERS • PHILADELPHIA

A man dressed in traditional German clothing takes part in an Oktoberfest celebration. The celebration originated in Munich, Germany as a 16-day festival. Today, Germans around the world celebrate their heritage during this time.

The German Americans

PEG ASHBROCK

WE CAME TO AMERICA

MASON CREST PUBLISHERS • PHILADELPHIA

Mason Crest Publishers
370 Reed Road
Broomall PA 19008
www.masoncrest.com

First printing

1 3 5 7 9 8 6 4 2

Library of Congress Cataloging-in-Publication Data
on file at the Library of Congress

ISBN 1-59084-107-7

Table of Contents

WE CAME TO AMERICA

America's Ethnic Heritage

Barry Moreno, librarian
Statue of Liberty/
Ellis Island National Monument

Ethnic diversity is one of the most striking characteristics of the American identity. In the United States the Bureau of the Census officially recognizes 122 different ethnic groups. North America's population had grown by leaps and bounds, starting with the American Indian tribes and nations—the continent's original people—and increasing with the arrival of the European colonial migrants who came to these shores during the 16th and 17th centuries. Since then, millions of immigrants have come to America from every corner of the world.

But the passage of generations and the great distance of America from the "Old World"—Europe, Africa, and Asia—has in some cases separated immigrant peoples from their roots. The struggle to succeed in America made it easy to forget past traditions. Further, the American spirit of freedom, individualism, and equality gave Americans a perspective quite different from the view of life shared by residents of the Old World.

Immigrants of the 19th and 20th centuries recognized this at once. Many tried to "Americanize" themselves by tossing away their peasant clothes and dressing American-style even before reaching their new homes in the cities or the countryside of America. It was not so easy to become part of America's culture, however. For many immigrants, learning English was quite a hurdle. In fact, most older immigrants clung to the old ways, preferring to speak their native languages and follow their familiar customs and traditions. This was easy to do when ethnic neighborhoods abounded in large North American cities like New York, Montreal, Philadelphia, Chicago, Toronto, Boston, Cleveland, St. Louis, New Orleans and San Francisco. In rural areas, farm families—many of them Scandinavian, German, or Czech—established their own tightly knit communities. Thus foreign languages and dialects, religious beliefs, Old World customs, and certain class distinctions flourished.

The most striking changes occurred among the children of immigrants, whose hopes and dreams were different from those of their parents. They began breaking away from the Old World customs, perhaps as a reaction to the embarrassment of being labeled "foreigner." They badly wanted to be Americans, and assimilated more easily than their parents and grandparents. They learned to speak English without a foreign accent, to dress and act like other Americans. The assimilation of the children of immigrants was encouraged by social contact—games, schools, jobs, and military service—which further broke down the barriers between immigrant groups and hastened the process of Americanization. Along the way, many family traditions were lost or abandoned.

Today, the pride that Americans have in their ethnic roots is one of the abiding strengths of both the United States and Canada. It shows that the theory which called America a "melting pot" of the world's people was never really true. The thought that a single "American" would emerge from the combination of these peoples has never happened, for Americans have grown more reluctant than ever before to forget the struggles of their ethnic forefathers. The growth of cultural studies and genealogical research indicates that Americans are anxious not to entirely lose this identity, whether it is English, French, Chinese, African, Mexican, or some other group. There is an interest in tracing back the family line as far as records or memory will take them. In a sense, this has made Americans a divided people; proud to be Americans, but proud also of their ethnic roots.

As a result, many Americans have welcomed a new identity, that of the hyphenated American. This unique description has grown in usage over the years and continues to grow as more Americans recognize the importance of family heritage. In the end, this is an appreciation of America's great cultural heritage and its richness of its variety.

The port city of Bremen sits on the Weser River in Germany. The oldest seaport in Germany, Bremen became a hub of commerce about 1,000 years ago.

1 The Trip of a Lifetime

Elisabeth Knapke's dream was like many others in the early 19th century. She dreamed of free land, religious freedom, and a better life. By the 1800s, many **emigrants** began to seek relief from the poverty, famine, and overpopulation of Germany by traveling to United States or Canada.

After months of consideration, the decision was made. Elisabeth was going to leave everything she knew and loved. The sacrifice was great, but the dreams of the New World lured her. The chance to make a new start, to pioneer an uncharted country was a dream so powerful that she would leave her home, her family, and her friends to build a new life far away in a developing land. It was the trip of a lifetime.

Elisabeth was an unusual young woman. She made the decision to leave her country and travel across the ocean with friends and a family from her small village. Although of low birth in her village, she was exceptionally well-educated. She knew how to read and draw. She kept a detailed diary of her daily life and her journey to the New World.

It was "a bleak and miserable day" on the first day of Elisabeth's journey to America, and she suffered strong feelings about her decision to emigrate. She was coming to marry Bernard Boeke, a childhood friend who had immigrated to Cincinnati, Ohio, the year before.

Elisabeth's journey began in her hometown in northern Germany. She was traveling with friends to the German port city of Bremen. For eight long days, they alternated walking and riding in a wagon, starting early each day, taking only bread and eggs with them for that day's journey. The days passed slowly. "We learn again it takes time and patience" Elisabeth wrote. "This is just the beginning, and we know nothing."

Elisabeth, like her fellow travelers, spent the next 15 days inside the German coastal city of Bremen, talking with the representatives of various ships. After considering the costs and the **accommodations**, she decided to take a sailing ship to Baltimore, Maryland, and then finish her journey by wagon to Cincinnati.

She purchased a bed in a cabin that was the size of a sleeping alcove in her home and came with two drawers under the **berth** for storage. That was all the room she was allowed for her living articles for the nearly 60-day journey to America. Nor was she alone; she shared her room with seven others.

Elisabeth spent much of the 15 days before boarding talking with others who had made the journey. She learned about safety, what daily life was like on the ship, and what she needed to pack for her voyage. Passengers were responsible for their own food, cooking, and serving utensils. They also had to bring all the goods they would need for their new life in America.

Elisabeth and others boarded the ship and spent the night before departure on board. Early the next morning, the captain steered the ship up the Weser River towards the North Sea. Before crossing the Atlantic Ocean, the ship had to follow the North Sea, round the coastline past the Netherlands, Belgium, France, and England to pass out to sea. The captain tolled the bell as they began this extraordinary voyage at sunrise. It took three days to travel along the German coastline into the North Sea.

Elisabeth kept a daily log of her long and often dangerous journey, beginning

A German liner, the *Europa*, arrives at port on her maiden voyage to New York from Bremen, Germany. German immigrants, like many from Europe in the early 20th century, spent their life's savings for the cramped ocean voyage, with the hope of starting a new life in America.

with Day One in the North Sea. "The wind is powerful and strong. The ship trembles and rocks and twists from side to side, and then come great waves, end to end, and my stomach feels sick again. I have not eaten; I was so sick, as were all the other travelers."

Elisabeth and her fellow travelers were frequently seasick. Most immigrants of the early 19th century came to America on heavily packed wooden ships that pitched and rolled in the high seas. There was a constant danger of the ship being destroyed by the rough waves.

A man wears a traditional Transylvanian costume at the Oktoberfest in Munich, Germany. The style of his costume originated in the 15th century and was in daily use until the end of the 19th century.

During fierce storms the sailors who took their turns at watch were tied to the mast with ropes so they would not be lost at sea.

Safety was also the focus of the passengers. Threat of fire from candles or open cooking fires was constant. Disease could and did spread rapidly in these tight quarters, and there was little or no medical care. Some died during the voyage. The bodies were sewn into an old piece of canvas with a stone at the foot. All the passengers would assemble on deck, pray, and sing hymns until the body was lowered into the ocean.

Elisabeth's trip was eventful. "We must endure the shaking and the noise mid-decks, the children crying," her diary reports. "People are very much afraid, and alone. We cooked once in our iron pot. It is not cool here between the ceiling and our floor; the smells, the sweat, the smoke, and the many dirty people are revolting. The stench is dreadful, but the commotion more so."

The travelers encountered frequent storms. "Our ship was thrown sideways and back and forth at the same time," Elisabeth wrote. "The wind and constant motion, the uncertainty and fear, are continual." During the storms, cooking was not allowed—sometimes for days. Passengers and sailors then existed on **hardtack** and stale water.

Other days it was still. There was no wind, so the ship was motionless. This could also last for days at a time. During those long days of inactivity, the passengers' thoughts turned from their journey to their future. "We thought about our new fatherland, and discovered in our minds a counterstream of thoughts about our abandoned homeland," Elisabeth wrote in her journal. "The trip is costly not merely in money, but also in these contrary feelings."

The passengers traveled alone or in family groups, yet mingled with unfamiliar people of every class. There were no class divisions or social rank on board except that determined by what size cabin was purchased for the voyage. Those with the most money purchased larger, more spacious cabins and were able to establish some privacy. Most travelers weren't that fortunate. They were packed together in tight, cramped quarters, and only occasionally were they allowed to go on deck during calm days.

Elisabeth's journey was a long one. It was 54 days later that they saw the distant outlines of land for the first time, according to her journal entries. "This morning we saw land for the first time, thank God. Around 12 o'clock a pilot ship came and took us in escort to Baltimore, and in an hour we saw the long-craved-for land. Our goal is now here."

After fighting strong headwinds, the ship finally moved up the channel toward the shallower water and the entrance to the port. The anchor was dropped, and the police and a doctor came on to visit. "Not a single person on our ship was sick, and no one had died during our voyage," Elisabeth wrote. Her experience was not typical.

American inspectors boarded all arriving ships and checked the passengers. The rich, as well as the obviously ill, could leave when the ship docked. The poor had to take ferryboats to the inspection station to be examined. The United States didn't accept people with serious health problems; they were sent back to their old homes. Many immigrants didn't speak English and didn't understand what was happening.

With chalk, doctors wrote letters on the clothes of anyone who seemed sick. They paid extra attention to the marked people. Children with common diseases like measles were sent to the hospital. At every station, immigrants dreaded the eye exam. Doctors looked for *trachoma*, an eye disease that caused blindness.

The immigrants had to answer questions, as the government had just recently begun to keep statistics on immigration. They were asked where they were from and how much money they had. Officials wrote

PACKING LIST FOR AMERICA

Few lists of the items that immigrants brought with them to America exist today, but in her diary, Elisabeth Knapke included the list that both she and Bernard brought, as well as their seed list to start their American farm.

In addition to what he was wearing, Bernard's list included: shirt, pants, suspenders, nightshirt, wool coat, gloves, snow boots, handkerchief, chewing tobacco, iron needle, crucifix, prayer book, bottle of holy water, baptismal certificate and other personal papers, soap, cream, drinking cup. In his trunk he packed books, bed linen, lamp, sealing wax and seal, pliers, mallet, scissors, twine, tacks, spoon, knife, kettle, plate, pillows, leather apron, and medicine. On Bernard's food list he packed sugar, flour, salt, bacon, bread, rice, beans, potatoes, lard, sauerkraut, honey, and chocolate wafers.

In addition to what she was wearing, Elisabeth's lists included: long underwear, woolen petticoat, apron, nightgown, dress, coat, gloves, handkerchief, snow boots, candles, drinking cup, baptismal certificate and personal papers. In her trunk, she packed books, mirror, bed linen, paper, ink in bottle with stopper, pillows, blankets, purse, thimble, buttons, cotton thread, silk thread, yarn, needles, plates, knife, spoons, forks, and towels. She packed her foodstuffs as well: sugar, flour, salt, bacon, meat, bread, dried apples, rice, beans, potatoes, and sauerkraut.

To start their farm, Elisabeth and Bernard brought vegetable seeds: turnips, onions, cabbage, spinach, beets, parsnip, and carrots. Fruits included gooseberry, blackberry, strawberry, apples, cherries, peaches, pears, and apricots. They brought seed corn, oats, wheat, clover, barley, rye, and flowers, especially Elisabeth's favorites: margarita, snapdragon, peonies, lady slipper, morning glory, tulip, and crocus.

These two pages are from the journal of German traveller Prince
Maximilian Alexander Philipp von Wied-Neuwield, who explored North
America accompanied by artist Karl Bodmer. The page on the right depicts
an example of Native American art as painted onto an animal skin.

notes about their hometowns, families, and jobs.

The United States wanted people who could take care of themselves. Helpers translated the many questions and answers. Within a day, most people received a landing card that allowed them to leave.

Immigrants who failed inspection had to stay in the ports at the immigration centers until a ship took them back overseas. Women and children who passed inspection were not allowed to leave until a man from the family met them or sent a letter or a ticket for them. They waited days, weeks, and even months before they were allowed to leave.

Elisabeth's experience was different. She had money, a destination, and someone to meet her. "This trip is a powerful, profound experience for me. The first impression as I saw America: It is a joyful sight and a lovely land."

Elisabeth's trunks were unloaded from the ship and brought up on shore. "My heart rejoiced. It is now time to resume my journey to meet Bernard in Ohio."

This is the view from Heidelberg Castle, which overlooks a scenic city in the Rhine River Valley that dates back to Medieval times. The modern state of Germany did not exist before the 1870s; until that time, the region was a collection of small states, ruled from castles like Heidelberg by noble families.

2 Leaving Home

From the earliest days of this country, people born elsewhere came to America searching for a better life. Some were fleeing **persecution** and political turmoil. Many came for economic reasons. Others came for the chance to start a new life unencumbered by old traditions.

Their experiences were as diverse as their cultures, and so were their dreams. Some became farmers. Others toiled in factories. Still others brought their talents as builders, businessmen, and artists. By settling new regions and cities, providing a constant source of inexpensive labor, and by bringing their unique forms of political and cultural history, together they contributed to the building of a nation.

Before the founding of the German Empire in 1871, no single country called "Germany" existed. Germanic Europe was a network of tiny states. The people we call Germans were tied not by where they lived, but by their common language, culture, customs, and heritage.

By the time of Christ, the Germanic peoples had started spreading over much of Europe. In later centuries, whole groups would uproot themselves from one place in Europe and move to another. The migration to America was part of this wandering pattern.

The first German to reach the New World was a sailor named Tyrker sailing on a voyage with Scandinavian sea explorer Leif Eriksson. Sometime around the year A.D. 1000, Eriksson landed on

Labrador, an island off the coast of Canada. However, the large waves of immigrants to North America would begin much later in history.

During the 16th and 17th centuries, Europe was involved in a series of bloody wars over religion, politics, and money. The region that today is called Germany was then made up of more than 300 different states. The people of the different states followed different religions, so wars soon erupted. Because of the tangle of political alliances that existed throughout Europe, this became an international war. Three decades of fighting, known as the Thirty Years War, fueled Germans' desire to emigrate to a country free from constant warfare. They looked to America as a land of religious tolerance.

In addition, as an agricultural people the Germans were tired of the natural disasters that had forced many farmers and vineyard workers to leave. Over the next two centuries, periodic crop failures would send waves of emigrants from Germany.

The first German-American settlement in the United States was founded in 1683 in Pennsylvania, and more followed in the next century when war again raged through the German states. That first group of Germans came from the Rhineland, the area that had suffered the most during the Thirty Years War. On October 6, 1683, 13 families from the town of Krefeld came to Pennsylvania. William Penn, an Englishman who had founded the colony less than a year ago, had invited them. He wanted to populate his land with European settlers. Penn visited the German states to encourage emigration, offering religious freedom and farmland. These first German Americans invited by Penn established a community called Germantown, which still exists today in Philadelphia.

An "emigration fever" had seized all parts of German society. Those in the lower classes—small farmers, agricultural laborers, servants, workers, and *artisans* were the most interested in leaving. Emigration to America started as a movement of families of agricultural background whose dream was to start a new life on American soil. In later years, German emigration comprised individuals mainly from the cities searching for work in the rapidly expanding industries in America.

A boy whistles as he shines shoes to make extra money for his family. Young immigrants worked nearly as often as older ones, since families needed all the money they could earn.

23

William Penn was an
English Quaker who traveled
to the New World and
established the colony of
Pennsylvania in the late
17th century. Many Germans
soon flocked to the colony.
These farmers became
known as Pennsylvania
Dutch (from *Deutsch*, the
German word they used to
describe themselves). Their
influence is still felt in the
central part of the state,
particularly around
Lancaster and Lebanon.

Two factors often caused families to leave their home: push factors
and pull factors. A push factor pushes you away from your old country.
These may be economic problems such as crop failures, low wages,
underemployment, and so on. A pull factor entices you to a new
country. These were found in America: cheap land, industrial progress,
high wages, and the chance to move up in society.

Many more German **peasants** followed during the 18th century.
The agents of shipping companies and recruiters for the American

colonies made extensive efforts to attract immigrants. They traveled through the Rhineland in brightly colored wagons. Those who had no money for their trip arrived in America as "redemptioners," or **indentured servants**. They agreed to work for a period of four to seven years to pay off the cost of their ship's passage. American colonial landowners came aboard the newly arrived ships to buy redemptioners in a system that was like temporary slavery.

By the 1750s, there were Germans in each of the 13 colonies, but most ended up in the middle colonies of New York, New Jersey, and

GERMAN-AMERICAN DAY

In 1983, President Ronald Reagan officially declared October 6 as German-American Day. This date was chosen to celebrate 300 years of German presence in America, honoring the contributions of German immigrants to the life and culture of the United States. It is a time of celebration, of raising awareness, strengthening a sense of identity, and pride in the contributions of German-speaking immigrants and their descendants to the building of this nation. The designation "German" is used in a cultural, not political, sense to include the German-speaking Swiss, Alsatians, Austrians, Germans from Eastern Europe, and German Jews.

In 1995, the United German-American Committee of the United States passed a resolution to "declare the period from mid-September to mid-October German-American Heritage Month." Most large celebrations and activities in the German-American community, such as Oktoberfests, concerts, exhibits, and other special events, frequently occur during this time.

Pennsylvania. Few settled in southern colonies, such as Maryland, Virginia, the Carolinas, and Georgia, because many were opposed to slavery on religious grounds. They also stayed away from the south because a free laborer could not compete with the slave economy.

The pace of German emigration slowed from 1790 to 1815, in part because of the Napoleonic Wars that engulfed all of Europe. They became years of *assimilation* rather than expansion for the German-American population. With Napoleon's defeat, Germans in rural areas again began to seek relief from poverty, famine, and overpopulation by emigrating.

Until about 1830, most emigrants sailed from the Dutch port of Rotterdam or the French city of Le Havre. Later, the German port of Bremenhaven became the main departure point. Bremen was referred to as "the suburb of New York" by the mid-19th century.

A few decades later, Hamburg attracted emigrants from eastern and southern Germany. During the 20th century, Hamburg became the chief port of emigration as large passenger-carrying steamships established regular routes across the Atlantic.

During the 19th century, religious persecution played a role in the push to emigrate. Passage of *anti-Semitic* laws in some German states during 1830 to the 1880s forced many German Jews to flee Bavaria to seek a better life.

A failed political- and social-reform revolution in 1848 brought several thousand Germans to America. Known as the "forty-eighters," these liberal, *agnostic* intellectuals were to have a

Under the leadership of Otto von Bismarck, the "iron chancellor," Germany grew from a weak confederation of states to a powerful empire. For most of the last half of the 19th century, Bismarck's policies controlled the destinies of most of the countries of Europe.

tremendous effect on German-American life. More than half became involved in journalism; many had edited or written newspapers in Germany. Most regarded the press as a vehicle for social change. Many worked to unite different groups around issues that affected all Germans in the New World.

A major wave of emigration hit the northern German towns of Westphalia and Hanover in the 1850s, peaking in 1854, when 215,000 people left their homeland. Nearly 1.3 million Germans left in that decade alone, including many highly skilled, well-educated professionals, such as doctors, lawyers, teachers, scientists, and industrialists. A second wave of German immigrants arrived in America in 1864, and within 10 years, another one million had come to America. Another heavy migration of Germans was from 1880 to 1893 when approximately 1.8 million made their way to the New World.

Upheaval in Germany caused much of the mass emigration. In 1862, Otto von Bismark became prime minister of Prussia. He was determined to unite the German lands under Prussia's leadership by forging a military alliance of German states. The Franco-Prussian War ended in 1870 with all the German rulers united into one German empire. Bismark standardized all the legal, financial, and governmental systems and launched a *Kulturkampf* (culture struggle) to reduce the influence of the Roman Catholic Church in Germany. German Catholics responded by emigrating to North America, where they settled in cities like Milwaukee, Cincinnati, St. Louis, and Alberta, Canada.

Most German immigrants between 1880 and 1914 were not from western Europe, but from eastern Europe. Many left their homelands to escape mobs who attacked them because of their *ethnicity*, religion, or politics. These Russian Germans settled in the upper Midwest region and into western Canada.

Until 1870, 90 percent of all overseas immigrants had come from Protestant and western Europe. Many of these nations had democratic traditions and education systems. Even among the poor, many had spent time in school or had acquired some industrial skills on the job. A few spoke English. Many settled in agricultural regions and hoped to acquire land to start small family farms.

After 1870, these new arrivals came from eastern and southern Europe from nations that didn't have well-developed education systems or voting rights. They landed in a changed America, one that was turning away from agriculture to become a modern, industrialized nation.

Immigrant numbers to the U.S. slowed during the war years of the American Civil War (1861–65), the Franco-Prussian War in Europe (1870–71), and especially World War I (1914–18). In between, however, German immigration to America was massive.

From 1923 to 1963, the number of German arrivals on the shores of the United States still outnumbered those from any other country. During the 1930s, many were Jews seeking refuge from Hitler's anti-Semitic policies.

After 1945, another wave of German emigrants flooded the U.S. to escape the devastation caused by World War II. The post-war division

The slogan on a World War I propaganda poster reads: "Beat back the Hun [a derogatory term for Germans] with Liberty Bonds." After the United States entered the war against Germany and its allies, many Americans attempted to distance themselves from German culture.

of Germany into East and West Germany brought about a half million additional wartime refugees, most fleeing Communist East Germany.

Events in America served to divide further a German population that had already been broken up along religious, class, and territorial lines. Because they arrived at different periods and at a variety of ports, German immigrants settled all over Canada and the United States. Many stayed in the cities with strong German cultures: St. Louis, Cincinnati, Milwaukee, Philadelphia, and parts of the Middle Atlantic states and the upper Midwest. In Canada, they concentrated near Toronto and in Nova Scotia, British Columbia, and Saskatchewan.

In the three centuries since the first German-American settlement was founded, about seven million German-speaking emigrants have made their way to North America. They and their descendants form the largest single ethnic group in the U.S. today. ✸

German-born physicist Albert Einstein takes the oath of U.S. citizenship in 1940, along with his secretary, Helen Dukas (left) and his daughter Margaret Einstein. Einstein's theories of relativity led to entirely new ways of thinking about time, space, matter, gravity, and energy. His work led to such scientific advances as the control of atomic energy and to some of the investigations of space currently being made by astrophysicists.

3 Immigrants Find a Home

They came looking for a better life. From small towns and villages to the large, bustling, cultural cities of Germany, they traveled here to a changing America that was both parts frontier and urban center. These newcomers settled all over the United States and Canada, often deciding to live near others who shared their same hopes and dreams, spoke their language, and practiced a familiar religion.

Early in the 18th century, many German immigrants went to Philadelphia. In 1709, the government of England encouraged several hundred of them to go to New York by giving them land north of the city in return for their labor. A decade later, the French government attempted to colonize the territory of Louisiana by inviting German settlers to New Orleans. For the rest of the 18th century, German immigrants stepped off ships to begin their lives in virtually all the colonial ports, from Boston to Baltimore, Charleston to Savannah.

The majority of the Germans arriving during colonial times were farmers. They moved further into Pennsylvania, up the Hudson River in New York, and into northern New Jersey. A few went to New England, and settled in the Broad Bay region and along the Kennebec River in what later became Maine. German colonial farmers also settled in Virginia, Maryland, Delaware, the Carolinas, and Georgia.

After the Civil War, two of the major U.S. exports to Europe were cotton and tobacco. Cotton was shipped from New Orleans to the port of Lehavre, France, and tobacco frequently went from Baltimore to Bremenhaven in northern Germany. To avoid coming back with empty ships, the captains of these vessels took emigrant passengers, most of whom were German, back to the United States. Sizable numbers of these new immigrants moved up the Mississippi River from New Orleans or inland on the Baltimore and Ohio Railroad.

In 1843, the independent Republic of Texas invited a group of **Hessians** to settle in Texas. The next year, about 150 families arrived in Brownsville, a port on the Gulf of Mexico. They founded the city of New Braunfels, which later became the gateway for many other German settlers. Texas became part of the United States in 1845.

From 1846 to 1915, many Europeans entered the U.S. at Galveston, Texas. Promoted by Rabbi Henry Cohen and the large Jewish-American community, Galveston called itself the gateway to the Midwest. It proved second to New York in its ability to attract immigrants. Thousands of Germans also took the long sea journey around the southern tip of South America to reach San Francisco during the Gold Rush of 1849 over the next few years.

Expansion continued westward with the passage of the Homestead Act. German immigrants brought with them a hardy red winter wheat that could be planted in the fall and survive the harsh winters of the northern plains states. The newcomers used this wheat in the Dakotas, Nebraska, Kansas, and parts of Colorado,

An immigrant leaves the Ellis Island ferry, carrying her possessions on her back and in her arms. The papers in her hand are probably instructions of where to go or the names of relatives already living in the United States.

helping to turn the vast grasslands into wheat fields that would become the breadbasket of America.

Germans from Russia also put down roots in California, planting the grapevines that now flourish as world-renowned vineyards. Settlers from the Volga region centered on Lodi in central California, and Black

In 1683, German immigrants under the leadership of
Francis Daniel Pastorius founded the neighborhood
of Germantown in Philadelphia. Germantown was
home to one of the largest colonial printing presses,
and was also the summer home of President George
Washington in 1793 and 1794.

Sea Germans formed communities around Fresno, where they helped establish a raisin industry.

The largest number of German Americans took up dairy farming. The dairy belt included parts of upstate New York, Wisconsin, Michigan, and Minnesota, clustered around large cities so their cheese, butter, and milk could be delivered to urban markets.

In the early 19th century, most of the German immigrants were young, unmarried males. Later in the century, entire families made the journey together.

Well-educated Germans, some of whom had attended universities, fled during various periods—1819, the 1830s, and the late 1840s—when the German state governments sought to repress liberal movements that attracted students, teachers, and intellectuals.

The wave of German immigration to Canada saw large settlements in Ontario; the Maritime provinces, especially Halifax, and the Annapolis Valley in Nova Scotia; along the St. Lawrence River; in Quebec; and in Toronto. Western Canada's German settlement occurred in the late 19th century with miners following the gold rush to settle in Alberta and Saskatchewan.

The process of emigration could be difficult. The German states required all family members to obtain emigration *visas*. Emigrants had to provide such documents as baptismal and marriage certificates from their local church, evidence of having a trade or profession, and proof that adult males had fulfilled their military service. Charitable organizations, in cooperation with governmental agencies, sometimes supplied emigrants with a travel guide, a map of the railroad lines in the U.S., and a list of German settlements where they would be welcome.

New York was the nation's principal port of entry for German immigrants. Some of Germany's charitable organizations established offices in New York to help newcomers. Baltimore was the second most-common port of arrival for German immigrants in the late 19th century. Other frequent ports of entry for Germans were the cities of Boston, New York, Philadelphia, Baltimore, New Orleans, San Francisco, Seattle, Mobile, and Galveston.

The German-American conflicts of World War I and World War II dramatically decreased German immigration as anti-German hysteria spread through the United States. Emigration hinged on the political climate in both these areas.

It was common for German immigrants and German Americans to move west with the frontier during the 19th century. German Americans contributed to the growth of such important midwestern cities as Chicago (opposite, top) and St. Louis.

Immigration from Germany fell after World War II. Most of the Germans coming to the U.S. then were escaping Nazi tyranny. By 1972, many calling themselves German were third-generation German Americans. ✳

A young woman works at a cigar factory in Pittsburgh, Pennsylvania. Manual labor was usually the only option available to immigrants, who often had little money and few connections to secure a good job.

4 Life in America

Fitting in or making do was the watchword for immigrants; they had to learn to change to fit the American way of life. German immigrants, however, would not give up their culture. Along with all the things necessary for their physical existence, they placed an emphasis on their cultural heritage, their language, their way of life, their personal concepts, their value systems, their plans for the future, and their hopes and expectations.

The German immigrants were a practical people. They arrived in America hoping to earn a good living as tradesmen, artisans, or farmers. Many came with their entire life savings, which often was enough to start a small business or purchase land for a farm. They chose their sites carefully. Businessmen looked for a good location in a neighborhood that needed their services, while farmers often chose land near forests that could supply timber for fuel and building.

People fresh off the boat were called "greenhorns." Farmers didn't stay long in their port cities. They set off as quickly as possible to stake a claim on land and then to start their new lives.

Those who stayed in the city were crowded into tiny apartments in tall buildings. Families often slept, cooked, and ate in one room. Their homes lacked clean air and light, and often also became their workplace. Many of the new arrivals could not speak English. Until they learned the language, their only way of earning money was to take in work at home. Whole families worked long hours for low pay.

In most families, everyone worked. Women and children rolled cigars, hemmed sleeves, or made brooms at home. They were paid by the piece. Some girls took jobs as servants. Many worked in factories. Boys worked for their keep in *sweatshops*. They shined shoes, sold newspapers, collected rags, delivered messages, or peddled peanuts.

More than most other immigrants, German Americans found jobs as skilled workers. Most had learned trades in their native land as bakers, butchers, brewers, tailors, barbers, carpenters, cabinetmakers, and gardeners, so they did not have to start at the bottom as low-paid, unskilled laborers. Some workers who had served as redemptioners to pay their passage to America had learned trades as *apprentices*.

Some immigrants demanded better wages and working

SCHOOL DAYS

During the 19th century, when children could be excused from their chores, they often attended school in crude, one-room cabins. Wooden benches lined the walls, serving as both desks and chairs. A smoky stove centered in the room was their only heat; their lighting came from oil lamps hung from the rafters. School days were long, and all the students studied together in one large class. Those who did go to school found children from a dozen different countries sat next to each other in class where they were taught to love their new country. They saluted the flag and played American games like baseball.

A girl in Bavarian costume pauses during a Children's Day festival in Germany. Traditional German dress often includes blousy shirts and suspenders or vests. These are usually decorated with jewel-toned colors.

conditions. They formed labor unions and organized marches and strikes. Bakers, tailors, and cigar makers formed local trade unions in New York, Philadelphia, Milwaukee, St Louis, and Chicago. In the 20th century, the growth of assembly-line industries created a new wave of labor organizing. Walter Reuther, a German American, became active in the struggle to organize automobile workers during the 1930s. He served as president of the United Auto Workers (UAW) from 1946 until his death in 1970.

During World War II—a war in which the United States joined with other nations to fight against Nazi Germany—Dwight D. Eisenhower served as commander of the allied forces. Eisenhower, whose family was German American, was later elected president of the United States, serving from 1952 to 1960.

German Americans dominated the printing industry, both as laborers and as journalists. As architects, German Americans played a significant role in the architecture of American cities during the 19th century. Where Germans settled, their style of design can still be seen in buildings today.

German immigrant craftsmen who settled in Pennsylvania brought with them styles of peasant folk art from southwest Germany. These folk craftsmen often painted their furniture, decorating it with colorful designs of tulips and other items. This style of painting is now called Pennsylvania German folk art. During the second half of the 19th century, large numbers of German cabinetmakers came to America to escape the restrictions imposed upon them by the European *guild* system. One result of this was the concentration of large numbers of skilled cabinetmakers in such American cities as Philadelphia, New York, and Cincinnati.

German merchants also opened taverns stocked with beer. In the early 1700s, breweries were established in New York, Baltimore, Milwaukee, Cincinnati, and in St Louis. By the end of the 19th century, there were hundreds, each with its own formula for making beer. The passage of the 18th Amendment in 1919, which made alcoholic beverages illegal, wiped out many of the smaller breweries.

The German immigrants dominated the industries of bookbindery and papermaking. They were carpenters, blacksmiths, and tailors in New York and Chicago; *cobblers* in the mid-Atlantic; ironworkers in the eastern states; stonemasons in the south; and they ruled the stockyards in Chicago and Cincinnati.

The relatively high-paying jobs enabled the wives of these German newcomers to remain at home in a traditional role. Relatively few German women entered the labor force except as teachers or domestic servants.

Many immigrants who arrived in the early 19th century were university graduates. They found jobs as teachers, journalists, and clerks. In 1914, Cincinnati had four daily German newspapers, four hospitals staffed entirely by German-speaking doctors and nurses, and more than 70 churches where the services were in German.

These newcomers started schools to preserve their culture and to keep their languages and religions alive. By law, children were supposed to go to school until they were 16. But many businesses posted "Boy Wanted" signs, and children often went to work because most families needed the money. Often, only the youngest children studied full time.

Schools held evening classes to help parents learn the language and customs of their new country. Older immigrants offered loans and advice to new arrivals. Rich Americans also felt a duty to help the immigrants. They opened settlement houses to help newcomers learn American ways. Part school and part neighborhood center, a settlement house usually had a playground, a library, a gym, and a kitchen. Volunteers gave classes in how to wash, dress, and cook American-style.

Within tightly knit communities, supporting family and adhering to culture was a strong bond. Preservation of traditional German dress, language, and entertainment was important even while adapting to their new country's own styles. Today, the Bavarian *dirndl* for girls and the white shirt and *lederhosen* for the boys are the traditional items of clothings most associated with the German immigrants.

They founded clubs like the Sons of Hermann to foster German customs and language to help financially needy members. Many other clubs, including social clubs, were formed in large communities. Some were associations of people from the same state in Germany; others were for specific purposes, such as the gymnastics clubs.

Equally popular were German singing societies. Choral singing was a beloved tradition. Sangerfests (singing festivals) were often organized

A man carries a clock on his back during an Oktoberfest event. The festival is a celebration of German culture.

in May and October, which feature a mix of German folk songs and classical music. Wherever Germans settled in America during the last century, they established choral groups and musical societies. Today, popular German folk festivals—the Oktoberfests, Germanfests, and Strassenfest—are celebrated in cities all over America.

German-born John A. Roebling perfected the techniques of building suspension bridges, developing the modern method of stringing parallel wire cables and of stiffening the bridges. His greatest achievement was his design of the Brooklyn Bridge in New York.

5 German-American Culture Today

German Americans brought to the New World all the cultural variety of their homeland. They touched America not only as individuals, but also as a group. They brought customs that are now considered part of the American way of life, such as food, culture, and even cherished holiday traditions. Today, 44 million Americans can claim partial or full German ancestry, making them the country's largest ethnic group. The real story of the German Americans is not so much what they have achieved for themselves, but what they have contributed to the development of the United States and Canada as it is today in industry, science, culture, military strength, and recreation.

Immigrants made lasting contributions to their new land. They gave the country its major religions: Protestant, Roman Catholic, and Jewish. Germans were the largest group in American immigration history to include sizable numbers of all three. After 1830, Jews from Germany began forming their own ***congregations***. German-trained rabbis, such as Isaac M. Wise from Bohemia, introduced the idea of reformed Judaism in the United States.

Immigrants had an enormous influence on U.S. agriculture. German farmers are credited with introducing the crop rotation system known as diversified farming and using barnyard manure, red clover, and gypsum for fertilizers. Pioneers explored the frontier with a

Kentucky rifle made by immigrant Germans. They traveled across the prairie states in a Conestoga wagon they designed and named for a creek near Germantown, Pennsylvania. Many immigrants were experts in such areas as carpentry, weaving, and **masonry**. Their places of work were workshops, not merely stores. German Americans have more than touched America's industrialization.

It's hard to name an industry that is not associated with German immigrants. From iron and steel to pianos and chocolate bars, all were German companies that started with an idea. German Americans founded major American businesses such as General Electric, HJ Heinz, Mueller's, Folgers, Bausch and Lomb, and Westinghouse. John Roebling came to America and began building bridges in the mid-19th century across Niagara Falls, the Ohio River in Cincinnati, and his most famous work, the Brooklyn Bridge. His major innovation was the suspension bridge, a roadway suspended from wire ropes. Ottmar Mergenthaler invented a machine that a printer could use to set a line of type in seconds. Before his invention, each letter had to be set by hand, and the process took hours.

Preservation of the German language was one of the keys to maintaining cultural traditions that united the communities. Not only were church services in German, so were classes in the public schools of Cincinnati, Milwaukee, and St. Louis.

American literature has been enriched by the works of such German Americans as Harriet Stratemeyer Adams and Edward Stratemeyer, a father and daughter who were better known by their pen names of

Thomas Nast became a political cartoonist for *Harper's Weekly* in 1862 and created such famous American symbols as the Republican elephant and the Democratic donkey. His cartoons attacked political corruption and public ignorance.

Albert Einstein is perhaps one of the most famous thinkers of the modern era. He developed the revolutionary theory of relativity and was awarded the Nobel Prize in 1921.

Carolyn Keene, Franklin W. Dixon, and Laura Lee Hope. Together, they had millions of readers for their series: the Rover Boys, Tom Swift, Ruth Fielding, the Bobbsey Twins, Nancy Drew, and the Hardy Boys.

Thomas Nast, born in Germany in 1840, was destined to become the most important political cartoonist in the 19th century. Nast trained his artist's brush on a polititian named William M. "Boss" Tweed, whose corrupt Tammany Hall organization dominated New York City government and stole millions of dollars from taxpayers. He also created the popular images of Santa Claus, the Democratic donkey, and the Republican elephant.

Education was heavily emphasized in German American families. Margaretha Meyer Schurz started the first kindergarten in the U.S. to prepare children for regular schooling. Gymnasiums and physical education programs, found in virtually every high school today, reflect the influences of the German-American Turners who started such programs of physical fitness in the 19th century.

German traditions are deeply embedded in the culture of the U.S., so much so that many people are unaware of their origins. The Christmas tree began as a German custom in pre-Christian times. It first appeared in America in Lancaster, Pennsylvania, in 1821. An evergreen tree, still colorful in winter, was a reminder that spring

GERMAN-AMERICAN LANGUAGE IN NORTH AMERICA

Henry Louis Mencken (1880–1956) was a journalist, editor, and literary critic in Baltimore whose study of language, *The American Language,* has become a classic in investigating the origins of distinctly American words. Mencken, a German-American himself, took a considerable interest in the German-American cultural heritage. He was one of the first to discover that many German words have found their way into American vocabulary.

Some of the following words are German in origin, but are now so common in American English that they are considered part of the American language: beer garden, stein, spritz, gestalt, angst, flak, concertmaster, waltz, yodel, zigzag, kaput, wanderlust, iceberg, kindergarten, Kris Kringle, paraffin, plunder, and cookbook.

Theoretical physicist Julius Robert Oppenheimer, educated in America, England, and Germany, helped develop the technology needed to create the atomic bomb during World War II. He studied quantum theory and the energy processes of subatomic particles, and his most famous work, the Manhattan Project, changed the face of modern warfare.

would one day come. Germans decorated their trees with candy, fruit, and gingerbread.

Easter is another holiday influenced by German culture. Coloring of eggs began in the Middle Ages as a special treat at Easter because Christians were not allowed to eat eggs during the religious season of Lent. The hare, or rabbit, became a symbol of Easter because the Christian holiday of Easter is celebrated on the Sunday after the first full moon of spring. Pennsylvanian children built nests in the fields for the Easter hare, believing that if they were good the hare would lay eggs in the nest. On Easter, the children went into their fields with baskets to collect the eggs, which had been set out by their parents.

German music served to unite both the old country and the new with works from Bach, Mozart, Heiden, Beethoven, Schubert, Brahms, and Wagner. Painters such as Albert Bierstadt, architects Walter Gropious and Ludwig Mies van der Rohe, photographer Albert Eisenstadt, and movie director Billy Wilder all have German ancestry.

Scientists such as the great Albert Einstein, Otto Klemperer, Eric Leinsdorf, Arnold Schoenberg, and Artur Schnabel were refugees who relocated to America and helped forge our scientific heritage. J. Robert Oppenheimer and Wernher von Braun, called the "rocket men," were scientists who created a partnership between government and science in the nuclear age.

Today, the highest percentage of German Americans live in Wisconsin, followed by North and South Dakota, Nebraska, Iowa, and Minnesota. In the most recent census, 23 percent of Americans claimed to be of German ancestry.

Famous German Americans

JOURNALISTS/AUTHORS
Thomas Nast
Theodore Dreiser
John Steinbeck
Sylvia Plath
Kurt Vonnegut
Thomas Wolfe

SCIENTISTS
Albert Einstein
Otto Klemperer
Eric Leinsdorf
Arnold Schoenberg
Artur Schnabel
J. Robert Oppenheimer
Wernher von Braun

BUSINESS OWNERS/ENTREPRENEURS
William Rittenhouse
Charles Steinmetz
Milton Hershey
Henry and Clement Studebaker
Walter Chrysler
Isaac Singer
George Westinghouse
Thomas Astor
Frederick Weyerhaeuser
Molly Pitcher
Mary Ludwig
Estee Lauder

ENTERTAINERS
Lawrence Welk
Florenz Ziegfeld
Oscar Hammerstein II
Walt Disney
Johnny Weissmuller
Fred Astaire

SPORTS
George Herman "Babe" Ruth

Casey Stengel

Roger Staubach

Bret Saberhagen

Lou Gehrig

Gertrude Ederle

ARTISTS
Ludwig Mies van der Rohe

Albert Eisenstadt

Billy Wilder

Emmanuel Leutze

John Roebling

EDUCATORS
Johns Hopkins

Paul Tillich

Bruno Bettelheim

Margaretha Meyer Schurz

WAR HEROES
Captain Eddie Rickenbacker

General Dwight David Eisenhower

STATESMEN
Herbert Hoover

Henry Kissinger

Glossary

Accommodations lodging, food, and services.

Agnostic not committed to believing in the existence or nonexistence of God.

Anti-Semitism hostility toward or discrimination against Jews as a religious, ethnic, or racial group.

Apprentice one who is learning a trade or art by practicing under skilled workers.

Artisan someone who specializes in a craft or trade.

Assimilation the absorption of a culture or group into a larger body.

Berth a place to sit or sleep on a ship.

Cobbler a person who makes and mends shoes and other leather goods.

Congregation a group of people who meet for worship and religious instruction.

Emigrant someone who leaves his or her native country to start a new life in a new country.

Ethnicity an affiliation or quality of a particular ethnic group.

Guild a medieval association of artists and craftsmen.

Hardtack a cracker-like biscuit made of flour, salt, and water.

Hessian a German mercenary serving in the British forces during the American Revolution.

Indentured servant a person who is bound by an agreement to work for another for a specified time, usually in return for payment of travel and living expenses.

Masonry the act of making bricks.

Peasant apoor agricultural worker in Europe, or member of the lowest class.

Persecution the act of harassing someone because of his or her beliefs.

Sweatshop a workplace that is often overcrowded and unhealthy where workers often earn low wages.

Trachoma a contagious bacterial eye disease.

Visa a stamp on a passport indicating that a person has permission to enter a country.

Further Reading

Galicich, Anne. *The German Americans*. New York: Chelsea House Publishers, 1996.

Hoobler, Thomas and Dorothy Hoobler. *German American Family Album*. New York: Oxford University Press, 1996.

Katz, William Loren. *A History of Multicultural America: the Great Migrations 1800s–1912*. Austin: Raintree Steck-Vaughn Publishers, 1996.

Magocss, Paul R. *The Encyclopedia of Canada's Peoples*. Toronto, Canada. 1998.

Reimers, David, and Sandra Stotsky, editors. *A Land of Immigrants*. New York: Harvard University Graduate School of Education, 1996.

Whitman, Sylvia. *Immigrant Children: Picture of the American Past*. Minneapolis: Carolrhoda Books, 2000.

Tracing Your German-American Ancestors

Carmack, Sharon DeBartolo. *A Genealogist's Guide to Discovering Your Immigrant and Ethnic Ancestors*. Cincinnati: Betterway Books, 2000.

Jones, George F. *German-American Names*. 2nd ed. Baltimore: genealogical Publishing Co., 1995.

Tolzmann, Don Heinrich, ed. *German Immigration to America: The First Wave*. Bowie, Md.: Heritage Books, 1993.

Internet Resources

http://www.census.gov

The official website of the U.S. Bureau of the Census contains information about the most recent census taken in 2000.

http://www.statcan.ca/start.html

The website for Canada's Bureau of Statistics, which includes population information updated for the most recent census in July 2001.

http://germanmigration.com/default.asp

This Web site provides information on the genealogy of German immigrants and emigrants, a search tool, and other resources.

http://www.germany-info.org

An extensive Web site sponsored by the German Embassy providing information about German events, politics, history, and economy.

http://www.ellisisland.org

This Web site is devoted to the history of Ellis Island and the immigrants who came through its doors.

http://www.ulib.iupui.edu/Kade/home.html

This Web site provides information and helpful links to German-American events and interests, studies, and more.

Index

Photo Credits

Page

2: David & Peter Turnley/Corbis

10: Bettmann/Corbis

13: Hulton/Archive

14: Adam Woolfitt/Corbis

18: Hulton/Archive

20: Corbis Images

23: Hulton/Archive

24: Independence National Historical Park, Philadelphia

27: Hulton/Archive

30: Bettmann/Corbis

32: Hulton/Archive

35: Bettmann/Corbis

36: Bettmann/Corbis

39: both Corbis Images

40: Hulton/Archive

43: Adam Woolfitt/Corbis

44: Bettmann/Corbis

47: Hulton/Archive

48: Hulton/Archive

51: Hulton/Archive

52: Bettmann/Corbis

54: Hulton/Archive

Cover images: (front) Corbis Images; (inset) PhotoSphere; (back) Corbis Images

Contributors

Barry Moreno has been librarian and historian at the Ellis Island Immigration Museum and the Statue of Liberty National Monument since 1988. He is the author of *The Statue of Liberty Encyclopedia*, which was published by Simon & Schuster in October 2000. He is a native of Los Angeles, California. After graduation from California State University at Los Angeles, where he earned a degree in history, he joined the National Park Service as a seasonal park ranger at the Statue of Liberty; he eventually became the monument's librarian. In his spare time, Barry enjoys reading, writing, and studying foreign languages and grammar. His biography has been included in *Who's Who Among Hispanic Americans*, *The Directory of National Park Service Historians*, *Who's Who in America*, and *The Directory of American Scholars*.

A writer of German and Irish descent, **Peg Ashbrock** has been writing her whole career, first in television journalism and now in books and magazines. She lives with her family in Cincinnati, Ohio. When she is not writing, Peg spends her days traveling with her husband, David, or carpooling and cheering her three children, Tori, Meghan, and Jon.